Little People, **BIG DREAMS**

ALAN TURING

Written by
Maria Isabel Sánchez Vegara

Illustrated by
Ashling Lindsay

Frances Lincoln
Children's Books

Little Alan was a boy from London who went to boarding school when he was very young. He was shy and nobody expected much from him. But often, the quietest people achieve the most extraordinary things...

At school, Alan spent so much time alone that he learned to read all by himself. He could also solve mathematical problems in his head before his teachers taught him how.

Everything changed when Alan met Christopher. They both shared a passion for maths and science and planned to study at Cambridge University together. Alan just couldn't imagine life without his friend… he had fallen in love!

He was ready to move to Cambridge when he got some terrible news: Christopher had died suddenly.

Alan – who had always been
lonely – felt more alone than ever.

University couldn't cure his broken
heart, but it kept his brain busy. Soon, Alan
was working on a crazy idea: a machine
that could calculate any sum.

Alan's design was the ancestor of the computers we use today, but he didn't have the chance to build it. Half of Europe had been invaded by Germany and Alan's destiny was about to change forever.

When Britain joined the war against Germany, Alan and other brilliant minds were hired to break the code used by the Germans to send secret messages to their soldiers.

Mathematicians, chess players, engineers… they all failed to crack Enigma, the code-making machine built by the Nazis. Alan knew that another machine — not a human mind — was the only thing to beat it.

Nobody believed in Alan's idea, so he wrote to the Prime Minister asking for help to build his device.

Once he got permission, it was just a matter of time before his machine solved the first of many riddles.

Alan's machine helped to win the war, and saved millions of lives!

But his name was kept secret and no-one knew he was a hero.
Alan was just happy to go back to work on his computers.

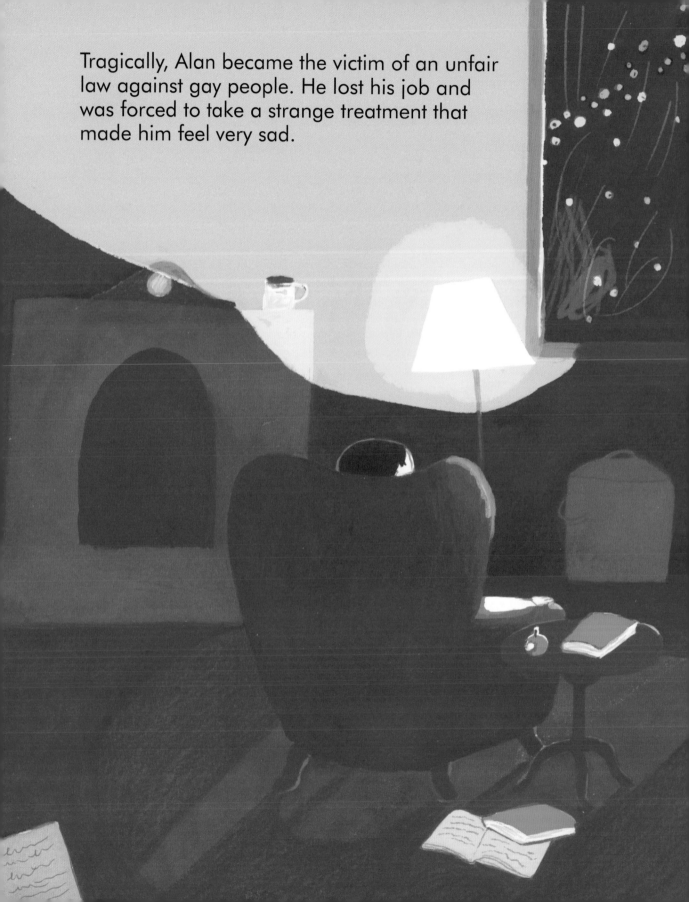

Tragically, Alan became the victim of an unfair law against gay people. He lost his job and was forced to take a strange treatment that made him feel very sad.

It took more than 50 years for the British government to apologise for treating Alan – and thousands of gay people – so terribly. They showed great courage by being themselves in a time of great prejudice.

And today, the world is much more open-minded thanks
to little Alan, the father of computer science. The boy
who believed that those who can imagine anything,
can create the impossible.

ALAN TURING

(Born 1912 • Died 1954)

1927

c. 1930s

Alan Mathison Turing was born in Paddington, London, as the second son to a civil servant, Julius, and his wife, Ethel. While his parents lived and worked overseas in India, Alan and his brother, John, grew up in houses across England. As a young boy, he was given a copy of *The Natural Wonders Every Child Should Know*, which quickly prompted an interest in the scientific world. Educated at Sherborne School, he met Christopher Morcom – a student in the year above with whom Alan fell in love. Christopher's sudden death aged 19 made Alan more determined than ever to achieve great things. Alan went on to study Mathematics at King's College in Cambridge and later at Princeton in the US, nurturing an interest

c. 1930s   1950

in probability and logic. He was already working part-time for the British Government's Code and Cypher School before World War Two broke out. In 1939, Alan began to decipher the military codes used by Germany and its allies at Bletchley Park. He invented a machine that intercepted messages sent by the Germans, which alerted Allied forces to attacks and saved millions of lives. Despite terrible persecution and prejudice for being gay, Alan went on to create the early modern computer in the years after the war. More than half a century later, Britain formally apologised for mistreating Alan and millions of other gay men who suffered in Britain. Today, Alan is considered to be the father of computer science and Artificial Intelligence.

Want to find out more about **Alan Turing?**

Have a read of this great book:

Code-Breaker and Mathematician Alan Turing (STEM Trailblazer Bios) by
Heather E. Schwartz

Brimming with creative inspiration, how-to projects, and useful information to enrich your everyday life, Quarto Knows is a favourite destination for those pursuing their interests and passions. Visit our site and dig deeper with our books into your area of interest: Quarto Creates, Quarto Cooks, Quarto Homes, Quarto Lives, Quarto Drives, Quarto Explores, Quarto Gifts, or Quarto Kids.

Concept and text © 2020 Maria Isabel Sánchez Vegara. Illustrations © 2020 Ashling Lindsay.
First published in the UK in 2020 by Frances Lincoln Children's Books, an imprint of The Quarto Group.
The Old Brewery, 6 Blundell Street, London N7 9BH, United Kingdom.
T (0)20 7700 6700 F (0)20 7700 8066 **www.QuartoKnows.com**
First Published in Spain in 2019 under the title Pequeño & Grande Alan Turing
by Alba Editorial, s.l.u., Baixada de Sant Miquel, 1, 08002 Barcelona
www.albaeditorial.es

A catalogue record for this book is available from the British Library.
ISBN 978-0-7112-4677-5
Set in Futura BT.

Published by Katie Cotton • Designed by Karissa Santos
Edited by Rachel Williams and Katy Flint • Production by Caragh McAleenan
Manufactured in Guangdong, China CC122019

9 7 5 3 1 2 4 6 8

Photographic acknowledgements (pages 28-29, from left to right) 1. Alan Turing, aged 15, at Westcott House, Sherborne School. © Alan Turing Institute. 2. Alan Turing, c. 1930s © Getty Images 3. Alan Turing, c. 1930s © Rex Shutterstock. 4. Electronic engineer Edward Newman Pilot Model ACE, designed by Alan Turing, 1950 © Jimmy Sime / Stringer / Getty Images.

Collect the
Little People, **BIG DREAMS** series:

FRIDA KAHLO

ISBN: 978-1-84780-770-0

COCO CHANEL

ISBN: 978-1-84780-771-7

MAYA ANGELOU

ISBN: 978-1-84780-890-5

AMELIA EARHART

ISBN: 978-1-84780-885-1

AGATHA CHRISTIE

ISBN: 978-1-84780-959-9

MARIE CURIE

ISBN: 978-1-84780-961-2

ROSA PARKS

ISBN: 978-1-78603-017-7

AUDREY HEPBURN

ISBN: 978-1-78603-052-8

EMMELINE PANKHURST

ISBN: 978-1-78603-019-1

ELLA FITZGERALD

ISBN: 978-1-78603-086-3

ADA LOVELACE

ISBN: 978-1-78603-075-7

JANE AUSTEN

ISBN: 978-1-78603-119-8

GEORGIA O'KEEFFE

ISBN: 978-1-78603-121-1

HARRIET TUBMAN

ISBN: 978-1-78603-289-8

ANNE FRANK

ISBN: 978-1-78603-292-8

MOTHER TERESA

ISBN: 978-1-78603-290-4

JOSEPHINE BAKER

ISBN: 978-1-78603-291-1

L. M. MONTGOMERY

ISBN: 978-1-78603-295-9

JANE GOODALL

ISBN: 978-1-78603-294-2

SIMONe DE BEAUVOIR

ISBN: 978-1-78603-293-5

MUHAMMAD ALI

ISBN: 978-1-78603-733-6

STEPHEN HAWKING

ISBN: 978-1-78603-732-9

MARIA MONTESSORI

ISBN: 978-1-78603-753-4

VIVIENNE WESTWOOD

ISBN: 978-1-78603-756-5

MAHATMA GANDHI

ISBN: 978-1-78603-334-5

DAVID BOWIE

ISBN: 978-1-78603-334-5

WILMA RUDOLPH

ISBN: 978-1-78603-750-3

DOLLY PARTON

ISBN: 978-1-78603-759-6

BRUCE LEE

ISBN: 978-0-7112-4628-7

RUDOLF NUREYEV

ISBN: 978-1-78603-336-9

ZAHA HADID

ISBN: 978-1-78603-744-2

MARY SHELLEY

ISBN: 978-1-78603-747-3

MARTIN LUTHER KING JR.

ISBN: 978-0-7112-4566-2

DAVID ATTENBOROUGH

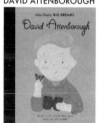

ISBN: 978-0-7112-4563-1

ASTRID LINDGREN

ISBN: 978-1-78603-762-6

EVONNE GOOLAGONG

ISBN: 978-0-7112-4585-3

BOB DYLAN

ISBN: 978-0-7112-4674-4

ALAN TURING

ISBN: 978-0-7112-4677-5